15028

The
Iroquois

The IROQUOIS
People of the Northeast

BY EVELYN WOLFSON

NATIVE AMERICANS
THE MILLBROOK PRESS
BROOKFIELD, CONNECTICUT

My sincerest thanks to Ann Hagenstein,
Dacia Pesek, Dorothy Tweer, William Wolfson,
Bruce E. Johansen, John Fadden, and the
librarians at New York State Library at Albany,
for research, reading, critiquing, and editing.

SERIES CONSULTANT

Karen D. Harvey, Ed.D.
Assistant Dean, University College
University of Denver
Co-author, *Teaching About Native Americans*

Cover painting by Tom Dorsey (no. 4743) courtesy
of the National Museum of the American Indian

Photos courtesy of: North Wind Picture Archives: pp. 11, 18, 27,
35, 39, 42, 44, 46; National Archives of Canada, Ottawa: p. 13
(C-92414 *Tee Yee Neen Ho Ga Row* by John Verelst); The Granger
Collection: pp. 16, 21 (left); National Museum of the American
Indian: p. 21 (right, no. 3524); Rochester Museum and Science Center,
Rochester, New York: pp. 23, 29, 33, 49; Trans. K10302, courtesy
Department of Library Services, American Museum of Natural History:
pp. 24–25; New York State Museum, Albany: p. 37; Photo Researchers
(© Peter Kaplan): p. 51; Jim West: p. 57.

Library of Congress Cataloging-in-Publication Data
Wolfson, Evelyn.
The Iroquois : people of the Northeast / by Evelyn Wolfson.
A Millbrook Press library ed.
p.   cm.—(Native Americans)
Includes bibliographical references and index.
Summary: Presents the history and culture of the Iroquois, from their
earliest years on the North American continent to the present day.
ISBN 1-56294-076-7
1. Iroquois Indians—Juvenile literature.   [1. Iroquois Indians.
2. Indians of North America.] I. Title.   II. Series.
E99.I7W82   1992
970.004'975—dc20   92-4642   CIP   AC

CONTENTS

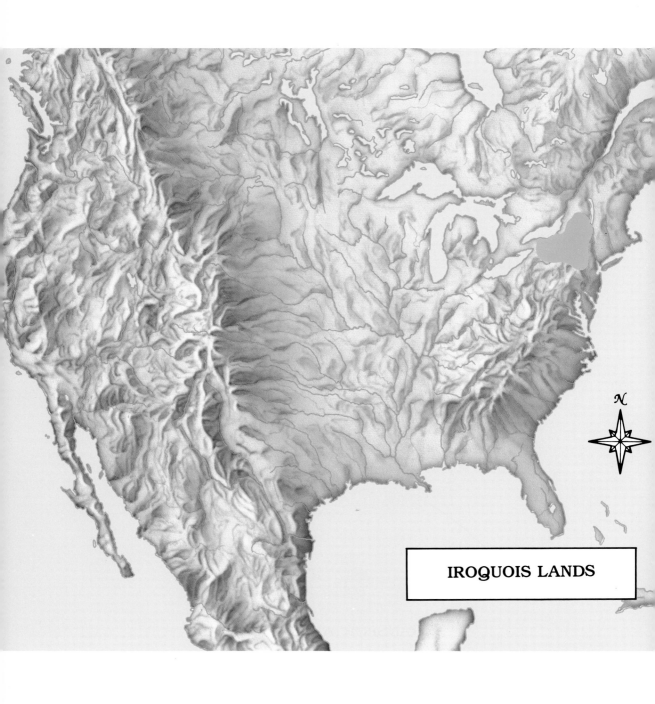

IROQUOIS LANDS

FACTS ABOUT
THE IROQUOIS

GROUP NAME:
Iroquois, or Haudenosaunee (hoo-dee-noh-SHOW-nee)
("people of the longhouse")

DIVISIONS:
Mohawks, Oneidas, Onondagas, Cayugas,
Senecas, and Tuscaroras (the Six Nations)

GEOGRAPHIC REGION:
Eastern and central New York State

LANGUAGE:
Iroquoian

HOUSE TYPE:
Elm-bark longhouses

MAIN FOODS:
Corn, beans, squash, wild plants, and game

TRANSPORTATION:
Elm-bark canoes

Chapter One

THE GREAT PEACE

Did you know that America's founding fathers were inspired by the Iroquois in their search for a form of government for America's colonies? Five warring Native American *nations* developed a set of laws to help rule themselves and solve problems. They "buried their hatchets" and formed a lasting peace pact long before there were colonies in America.

The story began a long time ago. The Mohawk, Oneida, Onondaga, Cayuga, and Seneca Native American groups settled in what is now upstate New York, in the soil-rich valleys south of Lake Ontario. They spoke a different language than the *Algonquian*-speaking Native Americans who had lived there before. No one is sure how they got the name Iroquois. Some believe it is an Algonquian word, while others say it came from French explorers.

In their new homeland the Iroquois planted huge gardens from the Genesee River in the west to the Hudson River in the east. Valley land nourished large crops of corn, beans, and squash, three vegetables that the Iroquois called the *three sisters.* Many freshwater rivers, lakes, and streams coursed over the land, and dense green forests covered the mountains and hills.

The only east-west route through Iroquois territory was along the Mohawk River, which cut through the Adirondack Mountain region. It was the main water route inland from the Atlantic coast. The Mohawks fought furiously to keep everyone else off the river.

DEGANAWIDA'S VISION ■ The Iroquois shared a long history of fighting with one another. When a person was murdered, the Iroquois believed in taking revenge. But sometime around 1450, the Iroquois underwent a great change. Deganawida, a Huron brave from north of Lake Ontario, brought a vision of peace to the Iroquois.

In his vision, Deganawida had seen a tall pine tree, a sign of peace. It had long, spreading roots that stood for spiritual unity. At the top of the tree perched an eagle, a symbol of protection. To Deganawida, this vision meant that the Iroquois groups should unite. He convinced Hiawatha, an Onondaga, to help him spread his message of peace.

By the mid- to late 1500s, the five nations of the Iroquois had united and formed the Iroquois *Confederacy,* also known as the League of Five Nations. (In 1722–1723 they were joined by a sixth Iroquois-speaking nation, the Tuscaroras, who moved to New York from North Carolina.) The nations agreed to join one another regularly in the *Council of the Great Peace.* They agreed to live under one great imaginary *longhouse* that stretched from the home of the Mohawks to the home of the Senecas. (A long-house is a long, narrow structure in which Iroquois families lived.) They would meet in the center of their territory at Onondaga, where the council fire would burn.

This symbol, or tribe mark, represented the League of Five Nations formed by the Iroquois in the 1500s. The confederacy, as it was called, was one of the earliest forms of government in northeastern America.

THE GREAT COUNCIL ▪ The Council of the Great Peace was modeled after Iroquois *clan* councils. Clans are large Iroquois families who trace their descendants to one female ancestor. At the time of the Great Peace, clans shared longhouses and elected the oldest female member of the clan to serve as clan mother. Three or more clans made up a nation, which non-Indians called tribes.

Clan mothers and the women of the longhouse chose a qualified young clansman to represent them in the clan council. The candidate's name was presented to the entire clan, which then voted to accept or reject the nomination. When a nomination was approved, the clansman met with other leaders in special council houses. The duty of these leaders was to settle disputes, set hunting boundaries, keep order in the community, and organize village moves.

After the Iroquois created the Council of the Great Peace, council clansmen chose *sachems*, or leaders, to represent them at Onondaga. There were fifty sachems in all. Nations with large populations chose more sachems than those that had small populations. For example, the Senecas chose eight sachems, and the Onondagas fourteen. But despite the number of sachems chosen, each nation received only one vote. Sachems served for life. But if they refused to attend meetings, broke a rule, or became ill, they were dismissed.

The Great Council concerned itself with matters that affected the confederacy. They discussed and voted on war, peace, trade, treaties, conquered nations, land issues, and tribal conflicts. Other representatives of the people, called pine-tree chiefs, also served on the Council of the Great Peace. Pine-tree chiefs were chosen by council sachems for leadership skills and speaking ability. They debated but did not vote.

Before the opening of a meeting of the Council of the Great Peace, an Onondaga sachem carefully swept the floor around the council fire with seagull feathers. An offer of thanks was given to the Creator and to plants, animals, the wind, the sun, the moon, thunder, corn, and other gifts of nature.

Speakers presented a string of shells, called a *wampum* belt, on which were designs that represented important information.

In the Council of the Great Peace, sachem was the most honored position of all. Here a sachem is holding a wampum belt, used to pass along important messages.

Purple wampum was made from the shells of quahogs (a type of clam), and white wampum was made from conch shells. The shells were cut into small squares, or blanks, and strung on sinew thread. The larger the wampum belt, the more important the message.

A brief period of silence followed each speech so that anything a speaker may have forgotten to say could be added. Then, the Mohawks and Senecas, who were called the Elder Brothers, discussed and debated the issues that had been presented with the Cayugas and Oneidas, who were called the Little Brothers. Each presented the views of their people.

When a vote between the brothers was evenly divided, the Onondaga sachem, who was also Keeper of the Fire, cast the deciding vote. No action was taken unless everyone agreed. Then a string or belt of wampum was hung on a horizontal pole near the council fire to ratify, or confirm, the agreement.

The Great Council meetings at Onondaga kept the five nations from fighting and ended a long cycle of killing. Followers of Deganawida preached the Great Peace to other nations, who also became united. But none were as successful as the League of Five Nations.

Chapter Two

LONGHOUSE LIFE

The people of the longhouse lived in a rich natural world filled with lush forests, cool-water lakes and streams, fertile soils, and many wild animals. Village life focused on the changing seasons. The rhythms of life were set by the sun, wind, rain, and snow. Clans listened to the land and responded. Life was tough, exhausting, and exciting.

VILLAGES ▪ Longhouses—Iroquois homes—originally looked like narrow, barrel-shaped wigwams. They were framed with bent saplings stuck in the ground about 10 feet (3 meters) apart in two long rows. Over the years, the houses were built taller and more rectangular. After Europeans came, longhouses were made with peaked roofs.

Some longhouse villages could fit inside a modern football field. These small villages had four or five longhouses, each the length of a school bus. Other villages were much larger, with many longhouses that resembled modern highway motels. These villages housed hundreds of people.

Clans protected villages by building them on hills high above rivers. Or they surrounded them with sharp wooden posts,

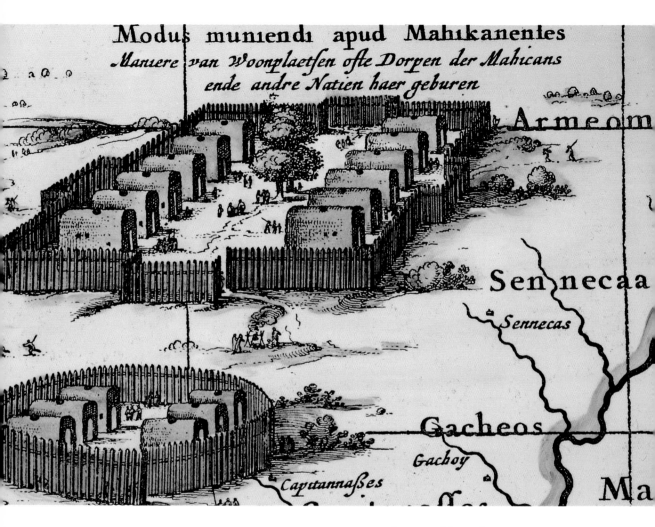

Early Iroquois villages were made up of longhouses surrounded by wooden fences built to keep out wild animals and other trespassers. Although the structures were solidly built, they were often temporary, since the Iroquois moved their villages when resources ran low.

called *palisades*. Gardens were always planted in fertile lowlands beyond the village.

The Iroquois moved their villages every ten or twelve years. When firewood got scarce and crops began to fail, the men went upstream to search for a new site. Once they found one, they burned the underbrush and trees in the area to clear it for settlement. They had to return several times to repeat the process. In a couple of years, the new site was ready.

It was time to pack families and belongings into sturdy bark canoes and paddle upstream. Men built longhouses and turned over the soil. Then women and children planted corn in the clearings. A new village was born.

DAILY LIFE ▪ In an Iroquois village, daily life was shared by large numbers of people living under the same roof. Clans used names like Bear, Turtle, Wolf, Snipe, Heron, Beaver, Deer, and Eel to identify themselves. They put animal symbols above longhouse doors to show which clan lived there. Men and women also scratched designs into their skin using pieces of finely pointed bone. Then they rubbed the designs with charcoal. Some tattoos were very fancy.

After the confederacy was formed, similar clans joined together. Bear clan members of the Mohawks became related to Bear clan members of the Oneidas. The Onondagas, Cayugas, and Senecas each had nine clans, and the Mohawks and Oneidas three. Children were born into the mother's clan, and when a man married, he went to live with the woman's family. Clan members never intermarried.

Animal names and symbols were used to distinguish different clans from each other. Animal designs were an important part of Native American decoration.

Inside a typical longhouse, a string of bunk beds lined the walls, and a row of fire pits ran down the center. The fire pits were 12 feet (4 meters) apart, the amount of living space assigned to each family. Sometimes a bead of light stole in through a smoke hole or an open door. Otherwise, longhouses were very dark inside, but warm. In the winter, cooking pots bubbled with strong-smelling stews. Smoke rose and fell in the warm, dark air. Families stayed in their spaces. For privacy they stacked bark containers between them.

Babies stayed safe and secure in cradle boards (a kind of baby backpack) until they were two years old. Then they toddled around, and everyone in the clan looked after them. Children played games and ran around the fire while adults worked and visited. They learned everything they had to know by listening to the rich language of their people and by imitating adults. They learned history and tradition through songs, games, and social events.

Adults made toys out of leftover natural materials. Parents folded pieces of thick birchbark into tiny containers and toy

The Bowl Game

Games of chance were played by all ages of Iroquois. In one, the bowl game, objects such as marked peach pits were given values and placed in a bowl. Two teams took turns thumping the bowl on the ground to make the objects fly upward. Each player caught the objects he thumped, trying to capture as many as possible. Beans were awarded for points.

Materials:

> A wooden bowl, approximately 12 inches (30 cm) across the top and 5 inches (13 cm) deep
> Peach pits colored red, green, and blue (1 to 6 of each color)
> 50 to 100 dried beans

Each color is assigned a particular number of beans. For example, red may equal 10 beans. Each team begins the game with the same number of beans.

Two teams sit opposite each other. The first person takes the bowl containing the pits and thumps it firmly on the ground. As the pits fly into the air, that person tries to catch as many as possible without changing position. Pits are sorted by color, and the appropriate number of beans is awarded. Then the bowl is passed clockwise, and each player takes a turn thumping. The game continues until one side wins all of the beans.

canoes. Men carved small wooden bowls for girls and dugout canoes for boys. Women made dolls from basswood twine and corn husks. Dolls were dressed in deerskin clothing.

BELIEFS ▪ Longhouse clans believed they were related to everything on earth, in the sky, and in the spirit world. Sun was an elder brother, and moon and thunder were grandparents. Everything in the universe had a spirit to be honored and respected. Happy spirits brought health and happiness. Unhappy ones brought illness and disease.

The Iroquois also believed that a force, or magic power, called *Orenda*, traveled through the universe. Orenda kept spirits connected and gave them energy. Orenda was responsible for such mysteries as lightning, earthquakes, and hurricanes. To keep harmony in the universe, the Iroquois made offerings and gave thanks to Orenda and the spirit world. Non-Indians came to translate this power into the power of gods or Great Spirits.

Festivities were an important part of community life. People came together often to hold rituals and celebrations. During some ceremonies, clans called on special healers and medicine societies to cleanse villages and drive away evil spirits. Healers could be either male or female, but only men could belong to medicine societies.

Healers made secret herbal brews by boiling the roots, stems, and leaves of plants in water. Herbal brews flushed illness out of the body and made people feel better. Healers also used herbal pastes and salves.

The Iroquois believed that dreams were very important. They believed that spirits brought dreams, which revealed a

*Masks carved from wood
or fashioned from corn husks
were used in the ceremonies of
healing societies. Today some
of these masks can be found
in Native American museums.*

person's hidden needs and desires. People described their dreams to healers, who prescribed special rituals in which dreams were acted out to release them from the mind. If a woman dreamed she owned a particular corn grinder, it was found for her. If someone dreamed of killing another person, that person's clothing was burned to relieve the dreamer. Acting out violent dreams in nonviolent ways helped the dreamer have peace of mind. And it helped the Iroquois to live in peace and harmony with one another.

Chapter Three

THE SEASONS

Village life followed the seasons. When the earth was covered with a blanket of snow, storytellers filled longhouses with images of giant turtles rising out of the sea, great horned serpents, witches, and stone-eyed giants. Stories reminded people of their history and brought meaning to traditional ceremonies. Children heard and told the stories so often they knew them by heart.

Midwinter celebrations, held in January or February, welcomed in the new year. Midwinter was time for renewing the mind and the body. Special healing societies held games and dances. Members of the False Face Society entered longhouses, danced around the fire, and blew ashes at people who were ill to drive away evil spirits. False Face Society members wore masks that looked like healing spirits. Members of the Corn Husk Society also joined in midwinter celebrations to thank and calm spirits of the harvest. They wore corn husk masks.

The Iroquois enjoyed playing games during annual celebrations. They often played Snow Snake in winter. Snakes were made from 6-foot (2-meter) pieces of flexible wood. Two teams, each with about eight players, took turns throwing the snakes across a smoothly prepared ice track. Snow snakes that traveled the greatest distance earned the most points.

The Snow Snake game was played in the winter.
The object was to see how far the long, spearlike
sticks could be thrown across the ice.

In the spring, sap from maple trees was collected and boiled over open fires. Maple syrup and maple sugar were the only sweeteners available to Native Americans until Jesuit missionaries brought sugarcane to the South in 1751.

SPRING ▪ In early March, villages bustled with activity as women moved their cooking fires outdoors and men prepared nets for fishing. It was time for families to listen to the land. When nights were still freezing and days were warm, families camped near maple tree groves and went maple sugaring. The job of collecting and boiling sap became an exciting game.

Spring was also time to gather tree bark to make new house coverings, buckets, bowls, rattles, canoes, and household utensils. While the sap ran, tree bark could be removed easily. Men collected elm, hickory, oak, and birchbark by making a cut all the way around the base of the tree and again 7 feet (2 meters) above ground. Then they made another cut straight up and down that connected the two circles. By gently working a wooden wedge between the tree and bark, they could lift the bark off in one large piece.

Sheets of bark reserved for canoes were spread on the ground and weighted down with rocks until dry. Small, sharp bones were used to punch holes in the bark so it could be sewed onto longhouse frames and made into containers. The sewing holes were filled and sealed with pine resin or spruce gum.

Very thick bark could be separated into layers. Men made strong twine from the inner bark of certain trees. Women used the bark twine to weave carrying straps, called tumplines, to support cradle boards, baskets, and containers. They wore the widest part of the tumpline around their foreheads or chests and wrapped the rest around the load.

Above all, spring was a time for planting. The Iroquois believed that long ago the Great Spirit gave people temporary use of the land. Women planted, weeded, and harvested the three sisters—corn, beans, and squash. Each clan cultivated a plot, and clan mothers directed the work. Land was never owned; the use of garden plots was passed down from one generation to another.

Broad grassy borders separated clan gardens. Families camped on the borders when they felt safe from attack. They also built tall watchtowers on them. Women and children sat in the towers and guarded the crops against birds and other animals. They sometimes snared a live crow and hung it by the feet, so that its flapping wings would frighten other crows. Traps were set around the garden to keep out raccoons, woodchucks, and deer.

*Native Americans used tree bark for many purposes,
one of the most important being the building of canoes.
The bark was carefully harvested in sheets, dried, then
stretched over the wooden canoe frame.*

When the leaf of the oak tree was the size of a mouse's ear, it was time to start planting. Women blessed the corn seeds, soaked them in water for several days, and planted them in mounded hills about 5 feet (1.5 meters) apart. Then villages held ceremonies to honor the corn spirits. Clans played games and gave thanks to the sun for warming the land and to thunder for watering the crops. People believed a job was well done only after spirits had been properly consulted and thanked because health and happiness came from contented spirits.

A few weeks after planting, tiny green shoots of corn poked through the earth, telling gardeners it was time to plant the bean seeds. Women planted pole beans around the bases of corn hills to give the bean plants something to climb. Then, when the beans began to reach toward the cornstalks, the women planted squash seeds around them to keep weeds off the hills. The three sisters shared the land and depended on one another just as the clans did.

Gourds were grown and made into lightweight, waterproof shells that served as cups, bowls, and dippers. Dried gourds with small holes cut in one end held corn kernels or small pebbles and made ceremonial rattles.

Clans also raised tobacco to smoke during peace negotiations and to honor the Great Spirit. Sometimes men sprinkled waterfalls with fresh tobacco leaves to calm the spirits inside the water. They also attached small bags of tobacco to masks to give them added power.

SUMMER ▪ While the crops grew, women and children gathered wild foods. Men fished, fought, or joined other Great Council

This fanciful painting, The Three Sisters, *depicts
the crops of squash, beans, and corn as three womanly
spirits. The sisters were thanked during ceremonies
in honor of bountiful summer harvests.*

The Three Sisters

The Iroquois planted the three sisters—corn, beans, and squash—together in one hill. Traditional longhouse festivals always included these foods. Corn is often served with deer meat (venison), beans, and a side dish of squash.

SUCCOTASH
(Onon'darha is the Mohawk name)

> 6 ears of slightly unripe corn, uncooked
> 2 cups shelled kidney beans
> Animal fat or salt pork

Cover the beans and salt pork with water. Bring to a boil and simmer slowly for half an hour, or until tender. While the beans are cooking, scrape corn kernels from the cob. Drain the cooked beans and add the sweet, soft kernels.

A modern, simple version of succotash calls for 1 cup of cooked fresh corn, 1 cup of cooked fresh lima beans, and 1 tablespoon of butter. Mix together and heat in a double boiler. Do not put in water and boil.

BAKED SQUASH

Put a squash in the ashes of a fire (or in a 350° oven) and bake until tender. Test the shell for doneness with a sharp stick. When it is soft, cut it open and remove the seeds.

sachems at Onondaga. In early June, villagers held strawberry festivals and danced in honor of earth's first ripening fruit. Many people believed that strawberries were sacred and lined the road to the Great Spirit, whom they would visit after death.

In mid-August, when the corn first ripened, women prepared for the Green Corn Ceremony. Corn spirits were thanked for bountiful crops and asked to return the following year. Dancers and musicians performed, and leaders gave thanksgiving speeches to honor spirits of the harvest.

Most celebrations included team sports. Men played a stick-and-ball game that French trappers named "lacrosse." Players carried sticks with curved ends that had woven nets used for catching the ball. The deerskin balls had moss and hair stuffing. Ten-foot (3-meter) goalposts marked each end of the field, which was 60 yards (55 meters) long. Men lined up, six or eight abreast, along their goal line. The ball was tossed into the air, and a player snatched it up in his stick. He ran with it or threw it in the air to a teammate while opponents tried to intercept the ball. The first team to get the ball through the other team's goal won the game.

Women played a game called double-ball. Double-balls were made by filling two small buckskin bags with sand and connecting them with a cord 3 feet (1 meter) long. The game required players to line up in a field between two sets of goalposts. Players carried long sticks with which they tossed the double-balls to one another. The sticks were also used to catch the balls by the buckskin cord that connected them. Opponents tried to intercept passes as the balls went from one player to another. The first team to move the double-ball from one end of the field to the other won the game.

Throughout the summer, while women tended the villages and gardens, men spent much time in the forests. Wood was needed for many things, and the men had to choose just the right trees. Although they had stone axes, stone was no match for hardwoods such as maple, ash, and oak. So they burned the wood first, to soften it. Men packed a thick layer of mud around the base of a tree to be cut. They left a portion of the tree exposed and then packed more mud above the opening. They lit a fire in the exposed area and let it burn until it went out. The mud kept the fire from spreading to other parts of the tree.

When the charred wood was soft and cool, it was chopped away with stone axes. Then another fire was set in the same place. The burning and slashing continued until the tree fell down. Burning took quite a bit of time, but it worked. Sometimes fires burned all day and night.

Felled trees were made into large dugout canoes by packing mud the length of the tree and burning and slashing it to hollow out the inside. Men also made wood into tools and utensils. They made burden frames, which resembled hiking backpacks, from flat pieces of hickory or ash wood drilled with holes for lashing. Almost every family owned a burden frame to carry belongings. Men also made cradle boards out of flat pieces of elm or ash wood. Women lined them with thick furs and laced babies in place using deerskin cords. Rattles, bones, and shells were made to hang from the board's bow to entertain babies.

After European settlers brought iron tools, men used them to turn ash-tree logs into thin splints for basket weaving. Oneida women became expert basketmakers, and ash-splint baskets provided income for many clans during the 1800s.

This early twentieth-century painting by a Seneca Iroquois artist shows a mother with her baby swaddled on a cradle board. The board kept the baby safe and secure while the mother went about her daily chores.

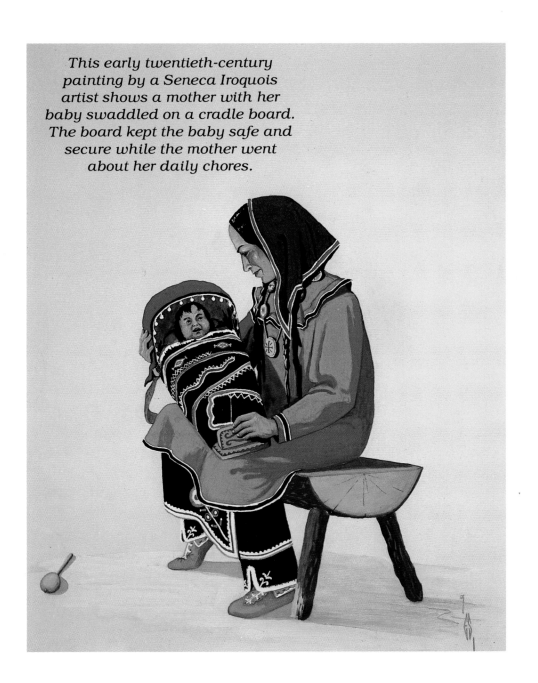

Women of the confederacy never became famous potters, but they made useful clay pots by coiling clay around smooth gourds. The gourds were burned away in firing pits, leaving strong but simple containers. Clay pots had grooves in the neck so they could be hung by ropes from tree branches and house rafters. Cooking pots had rounded bases so that food would cook evenly when nestled into hot coals. Small clay pots were also used to hold food in burial sites so that the dead would have plenty to eat on their journey to the Great Spirit.

Men made clay pipes with curved stems and open bowls. They molded figures of humans or wild animals on the bowls and wrapped clay around short pieces of willow to make stems. The willow burned away during firing. Men smoked pipes during ceremonial events when tobacco smoke was offered to spirits.

FALL ▪ In fall, women and children harvested and preserved corn, and men prepared to go hunting. Hundreds of corncobs dried on wooden planks so that air could circulate around them. Then women pressed kernels from the cobs into bark-lined pits in the ground below the frost line. Below-ground pits kept kernels fresh and protected them from hungry animals. Women also dried beans and squash. Squash was cut into thin slices and hung on long cords to dry.

The tough husks removed from corn were dried to make sleeping mats and lounging rolls. They were braided or rolled and sewed together. Women made a unique kind of mat from braided husks. These mats had ends sticking out one side to form a thick stiff pile.

While crops dried, women and children collected chestnuts, hazelnuts, hickory nuts, acorns, beechnuts, and butternuts to

Although it was women who traditionally tended the garden during the growing season, this sketch shows men helping with the corn harvest.

make flour. They also explored abandoned fields—collecting nettle, milkweed, and hemp plants to use for twine. Women stripped fine, thin fibers from along the stems of these plants and then rolled them with outstretched palms back and forth along their thighs. The rubbing and twisting motion locked the fibers together and made tough twine to weave into sashes, belts, and tumplines.

In the fall, men went into the mountains to track moose, bear, deer, raccoon, otter, and beaver. Successful hunters were greatly respected by their people.

Before hunters got guns from the Europeans, they used bows and arrows to kill large animals and tomahawks and snares to kill smaller ones. Sometimes they set deadfalls, which crushed the animals. Deadfalls were heavy logs or stones propped up so that they fell when animals touched a trigger.

Hunters sometimes offered the first deer of the season to eagles and owls or other birds of prey, putting the animal carcass high in a tree to show their respect for animal spirits. They took along tiny guardian spirits shaped from wood, clay, or stone to protect and guide them. These pocket-size spiritual guardians were as important to hunters as weapons.

Hunting provided more than food. The Iroquois wore simple shirts, pants, leggings, robes, breechcloths, dresses, and skirts made from deerskins. Women preferred to make clothing from deerskin because it was soft, supple, and lightweight. They cleaned the hides by draping them over a fallen tree and scraping them with an antler or bone knife. Afterward they spread the hides with softened deer brains and left them to soak. When the brain mixture was washed away, the hides were smoked over a small fire to close the pores—small holes in the hide.

Women made simple robes from thick bear and moose hides sewn together at the shoulders. Ankle-length moccasins had quilling and beadwork down the front. Sometimes moccasins went up to the knees and fastened with garters.

Animals supplied bone and antler material to make tools and ornaments. Bones were made into knives, spoons, scrapers, fishhooks, needles, and gouges. Deer-antler axes were used to chop away charred wood. Delicate bird bones were used for jewelry and whistles.

The Iroquois also made scrapers, diggers, spoons, and cups out of clam and scallop shells obtained by trade with people who lived along the Atlantic coast and Long Island Sound. They strung wampum beads, made from shells, into long strands or wide belts. Single strands were given to mourners after a person died. Sachems who had served on the Council of the Great Peace were remembered with many strands of wampum.

Wampum belts were kept at Onondaga, the capital of the confederacy, where they were cared for by a wampum keeper. Members of the confederacy used wampum belts to remind them of their people. Important clan sachems and elders read wampum belts from time to time to remind themselves and listeners of the stories associated with their design. Some wampum belt stories compare in length to a novel 150 pages long.

Ceremonial wampum belts like the one below were used by speakers at meetings of the Council of the Great Peace to tell stories or deliver messages. The design on this belt includes the Iroquois League pine tree.

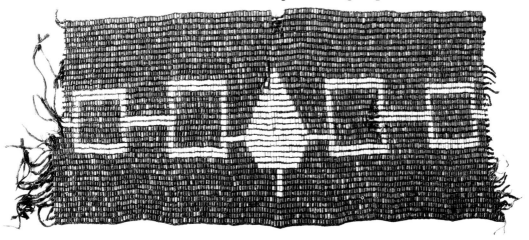

Chapter Four

TRADING AND COUNSELING

The Great Peace brought unity to the Iroquois League of Five Nations. But the Iroquois continued to fight with other groups. They tried to force other Native Americans to adopt the ways of the confederacy. They also fought to protect and expand their hunting grounds.

In 1534 the French explorer Jacques Cartier discovered that beavers were plentiful on the St. Lawrence River. Beavers had been trapped until they were nearly wiped out in Europe. The French were eager for new supplies of beaver pelts, which were in great demand. In Europe, it was popular for kings, queens, and noblemen to wear felt, or beaver, hats. (Beaver furs were made into felt by a process that fused the tiny bristles in the underlayer of the fur.) Thus the French, and soon other Europeans, began to trade with Native Americans for furs.

As more and more Europeans came to the New World, the confederacy competed with other tribes for supplies of beaver skins to trade for European goods. The French became trading partners with the Hurons, who were *Iroquoian*-speaking but not part of the confederacy, and other Native American tribes. The Iroquois Confederacy became trading partners with the Dutch,

*In the 1600s, the Iroquois traded with the Dutch,
exchanging furs for European goods.*

who had begun settling along the Hudson River. When the Dutch lost their land to the British in 1664, the confederacy became allied with the English.

To strengthen their bond with the Iroquois, the English created what they called a *Covenant Chain* in the late 1600s. The Covenant Chain described trade relations between the two nations. It called for the Iroquois to secure furs from neighboring nations and trade them with the British. In return, the British would supply trade goods, including plenty of guns.

The Iroquois preferred the quality and prices of British goods to those of the French and Dutch. But they did not like the British attitudes. The Iroquois would not accept the terms "father," which Englishmen called themselves, and "children," which the English used to describe Native Americans. The Iroquois chose to be called "brethren," a word that means equality. If the English did not use the term, they would have no Covenant Chain. Confederacy members reminded foreigners that they were guests on the land. To stay, they would have to obey the rules of the Great Peace.

THE ENGLISH AND THE FRENCH ▪ From the late 1600s to the mid-1700s, while members of the confederacy trapped and traded with the Europeans, Britain and France fought against each other in a series of wars known as the French and Indian Wars. They fought for control of the fur trade and the New World.

During this time, contact and trade with Europeans began to change Iroquois life forever. To be sure, some Iroquois families still listened to the land, gathered wild foods in season, and continued to fish and hunt. They clung to traditions they loved.

But many Iroquois no longer followed the rhythm of the seasons. Some families found it difficult to live amid two very different cultures. Few men remembered how to make stone tools. They had become accustomed to European-made iron tools. Tanning hides was a skill lost in the memories of very old women. Cotton and wool replaced deerskin, iron pots replaced clay, and shiny glass beads manufactured by Europeans replaced dyed porcupine quills. Men no longer hunted with bows and arrows or burned and slashed trees. Children played with dolls that looked European.

European missionaries brought new ideas of worship. Many Iroquois became Christian and attended Christian worship services. But it was difficult to follow both the ways of the Great Spirit and the ways of Christianity. Soon these many changes began to tear the Iroquois apart. The Great Peace, which had kept the Iroquois united for hundreds of years, became difficult to follow.

Contact with Europeans not only changed Iroquois life, but brought many dangers as well. The fur trade meant that the Iroquois could have many goods, such as iron tools, which made their lives easier. But it also gave them access to guns and alcohol. In addition, thousands of Iroquois died from deadly diseases brought by Europeans, such as smallpox and measles. And a valuable source of food, fur-bearing animals, was quickly being wiped out. Another problem was that the settlers were growing in numbers and illegally settling on confederacy land.

While the Iroquois declined, European settlers in the New World thrived. Thirteen independent colonies and many cities dotted the Atlantic coast by the 1700s. But while establishing

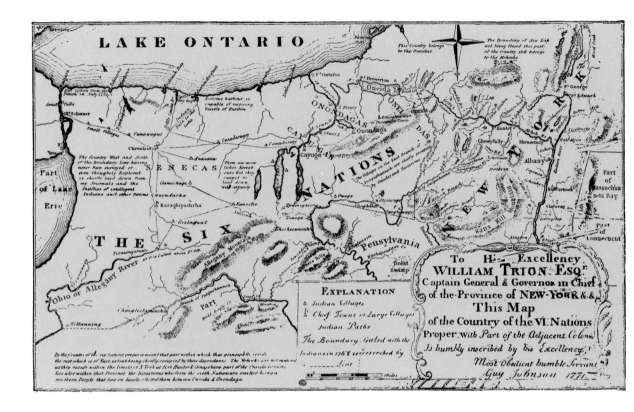

This map, drawn for Governor William Trion of New York in 1771, shows the locations of the six Iroquois nations before the Revolutionary War.

colonies, the British had neglected the fur trade. During that time, French trappers had allied themselves with the Iroquois Confederacy. So in 1744 the Iroquois and the English met in Lancaster, Pennsylvania, to discuss grievances between the confederacy and England's colonies.

It was a glorious meeting of two different cultures. Conrad Weiser, an Englishman who lived with the Iroquois as a boy, was an interpreter. He greeted the 245 Iroquois men, women, and children who came to the meeting. He served 300 pounds (136 kilograms) of beef, hundreds of loaves of bread, and plenty of rum. For two weeks members of both sides discussed issues of concern. It was the first time Englishmen had participated in such debates.

Before addressing the assembly, Iroquois speakers presented belts and strings of wampum. They said that they wanted *squatters*, or Europeans who settled illegally on Native American land, to stop taking their lands. They wanted the uncontrolled selling of alcohol to their people to stop. They spoke of the difficulties of trading with thirteen separate colonies, all with different policies.

Canassatego, the head of the Great Council at Onondaga, spoke well for the Iroquois. He had had practice speaking around longhouse fires from the time he was very young. Many of the Iroquois men spoke English. Their words were carefully chosen so that listeners would remember every thought. It amused confederacy sachems that Europeans could not carry speeches, or even sentences, in their heads. They had to put their thoughts on paper to remember them. Canassatego suggested that the colonists imitate the Iroquois Confederacy and unite to strengthen their stand against France. He warned the British that they must solve their problems and speak in one voice if they expected help from the confederacy.

Benjamin Franklin, a Philadelphia printer, reprinted hundreds of copies of the 1744 agreement between the Iroquois Confederacy and the English. He included Canassatego's proposal that the colonies unite in the same way the Great Peace had united the Iroquois Confederacy.

On their way to capture Fort Duquesne in Pennsylvania during the French and Indian War, General Edward Braddock and his men were attacked by 900 French and Indians on July 9, 1755. Braddock died of his wounds, and more than half his troops were wounded or killed.

By 1754 full-scale war between Britain and France was about to break out. It would be the last of the four French and Indian Wars. Colonial leaders called a great meeting in Albany to form a plan of action. Benjamin Franklin proposed that the colonies unite. He invited a Mohawk statesman named Hendrick to explain the Great Peace to delegates. Then Franklin proposed a plan of union—the Albany Plan. But it failed.

While Franklin was working to unite the colonies, he and other Englishmen negotiated for large blocks of Iroquois land in the Ohio Valley. When the French heard about this, they sent troops to the region. In the final French and Indian War, 1754–1763, England defeated France. During the war, the Iroquois Confederacy agreed to remain neutral, but individual Iroquois warriors often took sides.

THE IROQUOIS AND THE REVOLUTION ▪ The defeat of France spurred on the colonists, many of whom wanted independence from Britain. They were looking for new ways to govern themselves. They were fascinated with many Iroquois ideas—the free expression of ideas at council meetings, and council sachems who served the people. Many people greatly admired the Iroquois Great Peace. They compared it to the Magna Carta (an English document created in 1215 that guaranteed basic rights) and ancient Greek models of democracy.

When the Revolutionary War broke out, sachems debated endlessly around the council fire but could not agree to support the rebels. Nor could they agree to support the British. For the first time in the history of the Great Peace, sachems were unable to agree, and the council fire was put out.

Some confederacy nations fought on the side of the colonists. Other confederacy nations supported the British. One famous Iroquois who fought on the side of the British was Joseph Brant, or Thayendanegea. A Mohawk leader who as a boy was friends with many important Englishmen, Brant was very well educated. He spoke English and three Iroquois dialects. During the Revolution, Brant led many Iroquois raids against Americans.

As a colonel in the British army, Thayendanegea led the Iroquois forces against the Americans in the Revolutionary War. Although born a Mohawk, he was educated by the British, became a Christian, and took the name Joseph Brant.

The Revolutionary War ended in victory for the colonists. But the Revolution had brought much suffering to the Iroquois. Many of them had fought on the losing side. Many had been killed. Iroquois crops and villages were wiped out. And because they were on the losing side, the Iroquois lost much of their land. Perhaps worst of all, the unity of one of the oldest Native American confederacies had been destroyed.

After America gained its independence, the United States Constitution was created as the governing document. But people soon forgot that the Iroquois had contributed so much to shaping the government of the young country of America.

Chapter Five

A CHANGING WAY OF LIFE

After the Revolutionary War the Oneidas and Tuscaroras, who had helped the Americans, kept their land in the United States. Many Mohawks, Onondagas, Cayugas, and Senecas who had supported the British took refuge in Canada (among them Joseph Brant and his followers). The lands set aside for these groups were called reserves in Canada and *reservations* in the United States.

The Six Nations Reserve in Ontario, Canada, was not large enough to support a hunting economy and too large for women alone to farm. In an attempt to draw men into farming, Joseph Brant and other leaders purchased grazing animals and leased some land to non-Native Americans. But the non-Native Americans had a much better knowledge of the laws for buying and leasing land, and they took advantage of the Iroquois. Before 1900, more than 350,000 acres (141,750 hectares) of the Six Nations Reserve disappeared due to poor management.

Iroquois who had been loyal to the British but chose to stay in the United States were forced to sign the Treaty of Fort Stanwix in 1784. The treaty took away some Iroquois territory and set new boundaries for Iroquois land. By 1800, the state of New York and land companies eager to make a profit had pressured the Iroquois to sell much of their land.

Thus the Iroquois Confederacy was all but destroyed by the early 1800s. The Iroquois had lost much of their land and were scattered between the United States and Canada. And they had lost their livelihoods of hunting and fishing and farming.

On many reservations, men eventually began to farm the land, and the duties of the clan mothers disappeared. Married daughters went to live in small houses on reservations, and life became male-dominated, as it was in European society.

HANDSOME LAKE ▪ In the early 1800s, a Seneca named Handsome Lake brought hope to the Iroquois. He saw a vision in which spirits gave him a message of hope and guidance. The vision encouraged the Iroquois to return to the old values of kinship and family. Handsome Lake's ideas appealed to those who wanted to return to the old ways and to young people who had always lived on reservations and practiced Christianity.

Handsome Lake's message included a code that formed the Longhouse religion. Many Christian converts who had kept a strong belief in spirits and Orenda alive in their hearts adopted the new religion. They combined the old and the new. The Longhouse religion is still practiced in some Iroquois communities. Each week the Iroquois attend ceremonies conducted in their language and feel connected to their ancestors.

THE CONFEDERACY TODAY ▪ Reservation life offers little opportunity for jobs. Many Native Americans on reservations live in poverty. Thus many have chosen to look for work off the reserva-

*Handsome Lake, guided by a vision, preached
the Longhouse Religion to Native Americans eager
to regain some of their traditional values.*

tion, as lumberjacks and in other professions. Skills valued by
the confederacy allowed Mohawk men to become the world's brav-
est steelworkers. They could climb and walk, one foot before the
other, along narrow steel girders thousands of feet above water or
concrete. Members of the confederacy have become capable
bridgeworkers who have worked all over the world.

Today, the Saint Regis Mohawks, or the Akwesasnes, live on
land that straddles the Canadian–United States border. Between
1954 and 1961 the Mohawks fought and lost a battle to keep land
taken to enlarge the St. Lawrence Seaway. In 1969, after dis-

agreeing with Canadian officials who insisted that they stop at border crossings when traveling on the reservation, the Mohawks won the right to travel freely within their lands. Now, every year in July they celebrate with an annual Border Crossing Celebration to remind nations of their treaties.

The Saint Regis Mohawks also support a traveling college that visits Indian nations and teaches people about their history, and they publish an important periodical, *Akwesasne Notes*, that covers local and world issues about Native Americans. The Saint Regis Mohawks adopted the Longhouse religion and appoint hereditary leaders.

Eventually, many members of the confederacy who had settled on the Six Nations Reserve in Canada returned to their homeland in New York. The Senecas live on a portion of their original land on what is now the Allegheny Reservation; the rest was taken over for the Kinzua Dam in the 1950s. The Cayugas lost all of their land and are living on the Cattaraugua Reservation in New York, the Seneca-Cayuga Reservation in Oklahoma, and the Six Nations Reserve in Canada. They have a claim against the state of New York for the return of 64,000 acres (25,920 hectares) of land and more than a quarter of a million dollars.

The Onondaga Reservation contains the capital of the confederacy. It includes 7,300 acres (2,956 hectares) of land near the city of Syracuse, New York. The Onondagas keep confederacy wampum belts and maintain many old traditions.

A Mohawk child performing
a ceremonial dance.

Land disputes continue to erupt. In Quebec, Canada, in 1990, a dispute between the Mohawks and the local authorities left one person dead. And in 1991, the expiration of a ninety-nine-year lease of Iroquois land to residents of a town in New York State renewed tensions between the two groups.

Although members of the confederacy have lost much land, they have never lost their spirit. Population estimates vary, but some sources indicate that between forty thousand and sixty thousand confederacy members live in the United States, and a similar number live in Canada. And today the members of the confederacy who gave friendship and counsel to America's founders are beginning to be recognized as heroes of democracy.

AN IROQUOIS STORY:
TURTLE ISLAND

Native Americans had many creation stories that told how the land and its animals and people were created. Members of the Iroquois Confederacy have several versions of the creation of Turtle Island, or North America. This is one of them.

Long ago a couple lived high up in the sky. The husband was a great sachem who loved his beautiful wife and wanted to fulfill all her dreams. The wife, who was going to have a baby, dreamed almost every night. One night she had a most unusual dream. She dreamed that the tallest tree in the sky had been uprooted. When she told her husband, he thought for a while. Then he requested that six of the strongest sky warriors pull up the tallest tree. They tugged and tugged, but the tree would not budge. Finally, the husband grasped the tree in his arms and pulled at it himself. With one large sigh, the tree's roots let go their grip on the sky. The great sachem fell backward, and the tree and its branches and roots flew in all directions.

The wife peered into the deep hole left by the tree. She could see a dim reflection in the darkness below. She squinted her eyes trying to get a good look, lost her balance, and fell. As she fell, she clutched desperately at the tree, but caught only a handful of fruits and berries. She drifted downward as swans, otters, ducks, beavers, and muskrats gazed toward the sky in horror.

"What can we do?" asked Otter. "She has no wings. Her feet are not webbed. And her tail is not broad. She is not a water creature."

A large group of swans nodded to one another and rose silently into the air. They spread their wings until they were all touching one another. Together they made a low feather cloud that floated just above the water.

Slowly the sky woman came down and landed on the soft wings. The swans were pleased with their rescue. But they were confused. "Now what?" asked one of the swans. "We have saved her, but we cannot hold her up forever."

Said one of the ducks, "I know what she needs." And he dove down into the water, his webbed feet paddling hard as he went. The duck saw earth at the bottom but could not reach it. Again and again he dove. Again and again he returned unsuccessful. When the others had figured out what he was trying to reach, they volunteered to dive. "Let me go," said Beaver. Beaver dove down but could not reach the soft earth on the bottom. Discouraged and breathless, she returned and joined the others.

"Hurry," said the swans. "We cannot hold her up much longer!"

"I will go," volunteered a muskrat. And she dove deep down beneath the cold water. Muskrat was gone a very long time.

"Should we go after her?" asked Beaver, as the group flipped anxiously around in the water. No one seemed to know what to do. Then Muskrat surfaced.

"I have it! I have it!" she exclaimed. Clutched in her paw was a thick clump of dark, black earth.

The swans were baffled. "Now you have earth. So what? We are holding up this woman who is to have a child and still have no place to put her."

Just then a giant turtle surfaced from beneath the water. Her large eyes rolled around in her head, and her arms and legs flapped lazily back and forth as she bobbed toward them.

"Put the soil on my back," said the turtle. Beaver hurried over and plunked her paw-full of earth on the turtle's back. Then the turtle rolled her eyes upward and said to the swans, "Now put the sky woman on my back." Exhausted, the swans glided over and gently set her down.

The woman who fell from the sky was very happy to be able to stand up. She began to walk around in circles on the turtle's back. And as she walked, she dragged along the muskrat's clump of dark, rich earth. Slowly she opened her clenched fists, and fruits and berries fell beneath her feet.

Before long, Turtle Island grew bigger and bigger. Tall plants began to grow on the turtle's back. It became a snug retreat for the water animals and a comfortable refuge for Sky Woman, whose clan grew larger and larger. Turtle Island, the Iroquois name for America, is home to descendants of Sky Woman.

IMPORTANT
DATES

ABOUT 1450   Deganawida and Hiawatha form the Great Peace

1643   Mohawks and Dutch sign beaver-trade treaty

LATE 1600s   England establishes Covenant Chain with the confederacy

1722–23   Tuscaroras join the confederacy

1744   Colonists and confederacy meet in Lancaster, Pa.

1754   Benjamin Franklin cites confederacy model for his Albany
              Plan of union

1754–63   Final French and Indian War

1776   Declaration of Independence

1778   Mohawk Joseph Brant attacks American settlements

1779   Americans burn Native American towns and crops and
              break the power of the confederacy

1783   America wins Revolutionary War; Iroquois begin moving to
              reservations and reserves

1784   Iroquois forced to sign Treaty of Fort Stanwix

EARLY 1800s	Handsome Lake begins having visions that lead to Iroquois renewal and modern Longhouse religion
1969	Saint Regis Mohawks win right to travel freely across Canadian–U.S. border on their own land
1990	Canadian police storm a road blockade erected by Mohawks during a land dispute
1991	Ninety-nine-year lease granted to non-Native Americans to live on Allegheny and Seneca reservation land in New York expires

During the deadly dispute between Mohawks and officials in Quebec in 1990, supporters marched at a rally at Kahnawake Reservation.

GLOSSARY

Algonquian (Algonkian). The language spoken by Native Americans who once lived from Nova Scotia, in Canada, to North Carolina.

clan. A group of people who trace their descent to a common ancestor. The Iroquois trace their descent through the mother's ancestors.

confederacy. A number of politically united nations.

council. A group of leaders who meet and discuss specific issues.

Covenant Chain. The strong trading and military alliance between the Iroquois and the English during the latter half of the 1600s.

Great Peace. The constitution that served the Iroquois Confederacy.

Iroquoian. The language spoken by a number of Native Americans living in the United States and Canada, including the Mohawks, Oneidas, Onondagas, Cayugas, Senecas, and Tuscaroras.

longhouse. The long, narrow Iroquois house.

nation. A group of clans or families living in one region who speak the same language and share religious, social, and political beliefs.

Orenda. A mysterious force believed by the Iroquois to be part of everything in nature.

palisade. A village enclosure designed to protect against attack.

reservations. Lands set aside for Native Americans in the United States. ("Reserve" is the Canadian term for reservation.)

sachem. An Algonquian word, used to identify leaders.

squatters. People who settle illegally on land owned by others.

three sisters. Corn, beans, and squash.

wampum. Purple and white cylinder-shaped shell beads assembled into strings or belts and used to record important events and treaties. The word is taken from the Algonquian word *wampumpeag.*

BIBLIOGRAPHY

*Books for children

Arden, Harvey. "The Fire That Never Dies." *National Geographic* (September 1987): 374–403.

Basic Call to Consciousness. Rooseveltown, N.Y.: Akwesasne Notes, 1986.

Bruchac, Joseph. *Iroquois Stories.* Trumansburg, N.Y.: Crossing Press, 1985.

————, ed. *New Voices from the Longhouse.* Greenfield Center, N.Y.: Greenfield Review Press, 1989.

Caduto, Michael J., and Joseph Bruchac. *Keepers of the Earth: Native American Stories and Environmental Activities for Children.* Golden, Colo.: Folcrum, 1988.

Colden, Cadwallader. *The History of the Five Indian Nations Depending on the Province of New York in America (1727–1747).* Ithaca, N.Y.: Cornell University Press, 1958.

Coon, Carleton S. *The Hunting Peoples.* New York: Nick Lyons Books, 1971.

Culin, Stewart. *Games of the North American Indians.* New York: Dover Publications, 1975.

Everson Museum of Art. *Onondaga: Portrait of a Native People.* Syracuse, N.Y.: Syracuse University Press, 1986.

Fagan, Brian M. *Clash of Cultures.* New York: W. H. Freeman and Co., 1984.

Fenton, William N., ed. *Parker on the Iroquois.* Syracuse, N.Y.: Syracuse University Press, 1968.

Fitzhugh, William W., ed. *Cultures in Contact: The European Impact on Native Cultural Institutions in Eastern North America, A.D. 1000–1800.* Washington, D.C.: Smithsonian Institution Press, 1985.

*Graymont, Barbara. *The Iroquois.* New York: Chelsea House Publishers, 1988.

Grinde, Donald A., Jr. *The Iroquois and the Founding of the American Nation.* San Francisco: Indian Historian Press, 1977.

Grinde, Donald A., Jr., and Bruce E. Johansen. *Exemplar of Liberty: Native America and the Evolution of Democracy.* Los Angeles: American Indian Studies Center, 1991.

Hamilton, Charles. *Cry of the Thunderbird: The American Indian's Own Story.* Norman, Okla.: University of Oklahoma Press, 1972.

Hauptman, Lawrence. *The Iroquois Struggle for Survival: World War II to Red Power.* Syracuse, N.Y.: Syracuse University Press, 1986.

Jennings, Francis. *Ambiguous Iroquois Empire.* New York: W. W. Norton & Co., 1984.

———. *The Invasion of America: Indians, Colonialism, and the Cant of Conquest.* New York: W. W. Norton & Co., 1976.

———, ed. *The History and Culture of Iroquois Diplomacy: An Interdisciplinary Guide to the Treaties of the Six Nations and Their League.* N.Y.: Syracuse University Press, 1985.

Johansen, Bruce E. *Forgotten Founders.* Boston: Harvard Common Press, 1982.

———. "Native American Societies and the Evolution of Political Thought in the United States, 1600–1800." *Akwesasne Notes* 22, no. 5 (December-January 1990–1991): 7–9.

Kopper, Philip, and the Editors of Smithsonian Books. *The Smithsonian Book of North American Indians.* Washington, D.C.: Smithsonian Books, 1986.

Legends of Our Nations. Cornwall Island, Ontario: North American Indian Travelling College, 1984.

Lowi, Theodore, and Benjamin Ginsburg. *American Government: Freedom and Power.* New York: W. W. Norton & Co., 1990.

*Macfarlan, Allan, and Paulette Macfarlan. *Handbook of American Indian Games.* New York: Dover Publications, 1958.

Morgan, Lewis H. *League of the Ho-De-No-Sau-Nee or Iroquois.* New York: Corinth Books, 1962.

*Onondaga County Department of Parks and Recreation. *Onondaga.* Syracuse, N.Y.: Syracuse University Press, 1986.

Seaver, James E., ed. *A Narrative of the Life of Mrs. Mary Jemison.* Syracuse, N.Y.: Syracuse University Press, 1990.

*Siegel, Beatrice. *Fur Trappers and Traders.* New York: Walker and Co., 1981.

Snyder, Charles. *Red and White on the Frontiers.* Harrison, N.Y.: Harbor Hill Books, 1978.

*Tehanetorens. *Tales of the Iroquois.* Mohawk Nation via Rooseveltown, N.Y.: Akwesasne Notes, 1976.

Trigger, Bruce G., ed. *Handbook of North American Indians.* Vol. 15, *Northeast.* Washington, D.C.: Smithsonian Institution, 1978.

Vanderwerth, W. C., ed. *Indian Oratory: Famous Speeches by Noted Indian Chieftains.* Norman, Okla.: University of Oklahoma Press, 1971.

Waldman, Carl. *Atlas of the North American Indian.* New York: Facts On File Publications, 1985.

_____. *Encyclopedia of Native American Tribes.* New York: Facts On File Publications, 1988.

Wallace, Anthony F. C. *The Death and Rebirth of the Seneca.* New York: Random House, 1969.

Weatherford, Jack. *Indian Givers: How the Indians of the Americas Transformed the World.* New York: Crown Publishers, 1988.

Wilson, Edmund. *Apologies to the Iroquois.* New York: Farrar, Straus and Cudahy, 1960.

*Witt, Shirley Hill. *The Tuscaroras.* New York: Crowell-Collier Press, 1972.

*Wolfson, Evelyn. *Growing Up Indian.* New York: Walker and Co., 1986.

INDEX

Medicine societies, 20, *21*, 22
Moccasins, 36
Mohawk River, 10
Mohawks (*see* Iroquois)
Moon, 20
Moose, 35, 36

Nations, 9–11, *42*, 45, 47

Oneidas (*see* Iroquois)
Onondaga Reservation, 50
Onondagas (*see* Iroquois)
Orenda, 20, 48
Otters, 35

Palisades, 17
Pine-tree chiefs, 12
Pipes, 34
Pottery, 34

Raccoons, 35
Reservations, 47–50, *57*
Revolutionary War, 45–46, *46*

Sachems, 12, *13*, 14, 31, 37, 43, 45
St. Lawrence River, 38, 49
Saint Regis Mohawks, 49–50
Seasons, 22, *23*, 24–26, *27*, 28, *29*, 31–32, 34–37
Seneca-Cayuga Reservation, 50
Senecas (*see* Iroquois)
1744 agreement, 43
Six Nations Reserve, 47, 50
Sky Woman, 55
Snow Snake (game), 22, *23*

Spiritual life, 20–21, 26, 28, *29*, 31, 34, 36, 41, 48, *49*, 50
Sports, 31
Spring, 24–26, 28
Squash, 9, 26, 28, *29*, 34
Squatters, 43
Storytelling, 22, 37
Strawberries, 31
Summer, 28, *29*, 31–32, 34
Sun, 20, 28

Three sisters, 9, 26, 28, 34
"Three Sisters, The" (painting), *29*
Thunder, 20, 28
Tobacco, 28, 34
Tomahawks, 36
Tools, 32, 36
Toys, 18, 20, 41
Trade, 38, *39*, 40–43
Treaty of Fort Stanwix (1784), 47
Tree bark, 25–26, *27*
Tree sap, 24, *24–25*
Tribes, 9–11, *42*, 45, 47
Trion, William, *42*
Tumplines, 26, 35
"Turtle Island" (story), 53–55
Tuscaroras (*see* Iroquois)
Twine, 26, 35

Villages, 15, *16*, 17, 46

Wampum belts, 12, *13*, 14, 37, *37*, 43, 50
Weiser, Conrad, 42–43
Winter, 22, *23*
Women, 11, 17, 28, 31, 34–36, 48